Barefoot Muse
P R E S S

The Best of The Barefoot Muse

The Best of The Barefoot Muse

2005-2010

Selected and introduced by
Anna Evans

Barefoot Muse Press
2011

First edition, 2011
Published by Barefoot Muse Press

ISBN-13: 978-0615570730
ISBN-10: 0615570739

Printed in the United States of America

Acknowledgements

Thanks to my assistant editor, Nicholas Friedman, for his valuable help with the more recent issues. Thanks also to the photographers and artists whose work graced the pages of the online journal, and to all the poets who allowed me to publish their work, both here and online. Finally, thank you to my husband Keba and daughters Becky and Lorna for their patience and tolerance when I needed to work on *The Muse*.

Contents

Youth Politic   27

Only the Good   41

Literally Speaking

77

Forty-Two

91

Introduction

Poets are perhaps the people for whom the specificity of words carries the most weight, concerned as we are not just with definable meaning but also with connotations and associations, homonyms and heteronyms, stress patterns and aural qualities. And yet, often we make our decisions on word choices by intuition, realizing how apposite our inclinations are only when others point out some layer of communication of which we were not even consciously aware.

It was in this manner that my online formal poetry journal, conceived in the New Year of 2005 and delivered that same summer, acquired its name, *The Barefoot Muse*. I do know that there were some half-formed reasons for this choice swirling around my brain. "Muse" obviously originally referred to the nine muses of classical Greek mythology of whom no fewer than three were responsible for poetic art forms—Calliope, epic poetry; Erato, love poetry; Euterpe, elegiac poetry. Robert Graves later popularized the Muse-Poet relationship in his seminal work, *The White Goddess*.

"Barefoot" probably originated from a more complex and personally relevant phrase dating from the 1900s, "barefoot and pregnant", which was used in conjunction with the controversial idea that women should not work outside the home. In 2005 my youngest daughter was in kindergarten, and I was starting to consider my career options, limited though they were by my highly constrained fledgling-free time. I balked at the idea that retail or food service offered the most likely receptiveness to my skill set and résumé gaps, combined with the flexibility of hours that I needed.

In the end I went back to school to work towards my MFA in poetry, and started *The Barefoot Muse*. The journal became well known not only for its championing of formal and metrical poetry, but also for its willingness to publish poems on female subjects typically avoided by the formalist press such as breastfeeding—see Ona Gritz's "New Mother Reading"—along with poems which pushed at conventional barriers like David Landrum's "Shereen's Ghazal."

Looking back, I feel now that there was an auroral quality to my choice of *The Barefoot Muse*—I have a vision of a lovely nymph tripping across a dew-covered field. The metaphorical field I'm referring to is of course the World Wide Web. In 2005 there were far fewer online poetry journals and almost none prepared to publish formal & metrical poetry, let alone such poetry written with a subversive liberal slant. I like to think *The Muse* showed the way ahead, demonstrating to others how straightforward it was (although not quick or effortless) to run an online journal out of one's home.

And now the lovely nymph is tripping across another dew-covered field, though this time the field is Print On Demand publishing, a catchall label meant to communicate how straightforward it is, and even quick (although, again, not effortless) to produce and market a high quality book, available on all popular online retail sites, out of one's home.

The project, in addition to giving me the opportunity to reconnect with over fifty previous contributors to *The Muse*, and to rediscover the excellent poems I had selected for the journal, also allowed me to play with some more name choices — grouping the poems into short themed sections so that readers of the anthology could dip in as their mood inclined them. If some of these section titles seem idiosyncratic, forgive me — they are no more so than is the word "Barefoot" in the title of what has become Barefoot Muse Press. All of the connotations you choose to take out of the titles are probably true, even the ones I'm not aware of yet. The last section, entitled "Forty-Two", is of course the answer to life, the universe and everything according to Douglas Adams's *The Hitchhiker's Guide to the Galaxy*.

We should never expect any less of poetry than that.

—A.M.E.

Heart Trouble

Trouble

James Scannell McCormick

Who was asking for you that you've come knocking on my door,
And looking like a single spark in an August of no rain? You're

What follows *There's no easy way to say this,* you're the damp crack
In the cellar wall, the shadow on the x-ray, the one last martini before
                                                            driving back

Home on a slippery night. You've worked your wedding ring
Up over your knuckle and into your pocket (again); you're sliding

Down the bar towards me. Who was asking for you? You're as
                                                    unwelcome
As a smoke alarm's skirl, a whole side of the body gone suddenly numb,

A midnight phone call, a third straight night without sleep.
You're a bind, a bad way, a pickle, a fix: what I'm in, and deep.

The Next Morning

Juleigh Howard-Hobson

Hung-over, he was, facing down a strange
Shower, her shower, where the soaps were not
Just soap. Her soaps were lilac and a range
Of faded green and pink. *Pastilles*, the lot
Was called. *The pastilles are here*, she pointed
To them. *We don't use plain soap.* Dry, they felt
Powdery and light, which was bad enough,
But wet — wet — they slimily anointed
Him, leaving, as each one began to melt,
A slick perfume and nasty viscous stuff.

They're handmade with French herbs, she'd pronounced, and
Showed him where they were. Outside the shower
Stall. Her in pink robe, comfortable, grand...
Him in awkward nothing. Stripped of power
Aloe for your face, she said, *lavender...,*
 She stopped, giving him an apprising stare
... for the rest of you. And she'd turned to leave,
Then stopped again, adding the rejoinder
They're quite expensive, don't waste them in there.
And she'd left him. He wasn't so naive

To think he was supposed to stay once he
Cleaned up and got dressed. No, they were done. They
Met, she got to live out some fantasy
Or other about having sex all day
With the working classes, with no risk
That he would matter. He stood in the stall,
The water hot and rushing down like rain
Not washing, not moving. Letting the discs,

The *pastilles,* slip from his fingers and fall
On the shower floor and melt down the drain.

Nominated for Sundress Best of the Net Anthology and a Pushcart Prize

Gossip

Kim Bridgford

All the world may not love a lover
but they will be watching him.
Lucky Numbers 12, 34, 5, 47, 8, 19

We like to think the world's in love with love,
But actually it's more in love with talk.
We like to think the world's view is above,
But it is not—nor does it walk the walk

Of those who suffer, or go against all odds.
No. It's the heat of public enterprise
That fuels the traveling talk to fantasize:
He left his wife? How many hotel beds?

Tongues now begin to click, and ears to listen
For someone else who knows the body's heat.
For love is not just sex but moral lesson,
Depending on who's happy and who's not,
Depending on what is and isn't said,
Depending on who's watching up ahead.

On the Erotics of Deployment

Jehanne Dubrow

I'll build an altar
      to the tiny flecks fallen from his razor,

the pair of coveralls crumpled near the bed,
      the history of war he left unread.

The Goddess of Impermanence
      will be evicted from my home. In Her absence,

I will exhibit art
      composed of my vestigial parts,

my breasts the centerpiece
      to this display. I will be all of Greece

and Italy. I will forget about my skin
      and the awful need for friction,

how often I'm an empty plate.
      Or else, I won't forget but only tolerate

neglect. Some wives prefer
      to wait along the pier, green glitter

on their eyes, their bodies wrapped in scarlet.
      I'll try to be the harlot

that I want to be,
      Bathsheba gleaming on the balcony,

Susannah combing tangles from her hair.
        I will prepare

myself for him, a feast, a holy sacrifice.
        I'll be the fruit kept edible on ice.

from *Stateside* (Northwestern UP, 2010)

You Know What You Could Do for Me?

Deborah Kreuze

You know what you could do for me?
It might be something you don't get.
Apologize and let me be.

I mean a real apology,
The sort you've not attempted yet,
you know? What you could do, for me,

is simulate some empathy.
Acknowledge you've incurred a debt.
Apologize. And let me be

alone to purge this memory.
You think you couldn't now, I bet.
You know what? You could. Do for me

something you don't normally.
I want to move on and forget.
Apologize, and let me. Be

the jerk who made wild love to me
whose wife called me in her upset.
You know what you could do for me?
Apologize and let me be.

Shereen's Ghazal

David W. Landrum

A whore, I've this to tell: men want my cunt.
I travel the Silk Road and sell my cunt.

I lay down nights here under the vast sky.
Under the ice of stars, unveil my cunt.

Persians, Turks, and Arabs flock to me.
One joy unites this clientele: my cunt!

Christians, Zoroastrians make the pilgrimage.
They worship me, rush pell-mell to my cunt.

Soldiers, camel-men, rich merchants come.
See how they all grovel before my cunt.

I walk the mountains and endure dust storms.
I'm quite the belle — men love my pretty cunt!

Under the wagon, lamps burn, money clinks.
I'm laughing, rich as hell — my golden cunt!

Love Test: A Ghazal

Diane Lockward

The sign on the wall read: *Test on Love*
Coming Soon. "My God," I thought, "a test on love!"

I felt the familiar panic,
the tightening in my chest. On love

I'd be lucky if I pulled a C-.
I've always made a mess of love.

It's not as if I haven't tried.
Why, I've even gone in quest of love.

I've studied, done research, pulled all-nighters,
but I can't master the lesson. Love

and its meaning seem to elude me,
though I've given my best to love.

I trembled at the thought of the upcoming exam,
knew I'd never get the gist of love.

What if the teacher called me in front of the class
and made this request: "On love

please speak extemporaneously"?
I'd look like a fool when I confessed, "On love

I can't speak at all." Or worse, an essay question
demanding some new twist on love!

What if it were fill-in-the-blanks that required
memorization of the entire text of love?

What if my answers were stupid or trite,
seemingly given in jest of love?

Maybe I'd get lucky — multiple choice or true and false.
Then at least I could guess on love.

If nothing else worked, I could always throw up
a prayer: "Dear God, let me be blessed in love.

Don't let me suffer the shame of hearing,
"Diane, once again, you've received an F in love."

From *What Feeds Us* (Wind Publications, 2006)

Dipstick

Chris O'Carroll

The penis really is the dipstick for male health without any question at all.
-- Dr. Mehmet Oz on The Oprah Show

The penis is the dipstick for male health,
So Oprah Winfrey heard from Dr. Oz.
This overt organ practices no stealth,
But frankly flaunts all virtues and all flaws.
When it voids water in a robust flow
Or stands in readiness to drill and thrill,
Then the entire body's good to go;
This member well proclaims the team not ill.
But if it dribbles, falters, stalls, or sags,
The system elsewhere may be on the blink.
When this proud pole flies ominous red flags,
The *tout ensemble*'s no longer in the pink.
  Behold! The dipstick says my mortal coil
  Is far from shuffled off. Let's check your oil.

Family Matters

My Baby Fell Apart

Annie Finch

My baby fell apart, and I could see.
It was a simple vision of surrender.
There was no baby left inside of me.

I learned something alone when suddenly
The baby bent, in a way I could not bend her.
My baby fell apart, and I could see

Her falling through a loud internal sea
Away from the one place that still kept tender.
There was no baby left inside of me.

I came apart; I couldn't even be
There for the loss. I lost my need to mend her
When my baby fell apart, and I could see

Something of her who fell away from me,
But nothing to make me ever need to tend her.
There was no baby left inside of me;

I had no baby. I could only see
The need to be apart from her, to end her.
My baby fell apart—and I could see.
There was no baby left inside of me.

Since You Asked

Ona Gritz

Yes, Darling, it hurt. And don't you believe
for a minute I could forget that kind
of pain. Clutching hard at your father's sleeve,
I burned with it; on my sides and my spine.
I shook with sweat as you went at my bones,
cracking me open with hammer blows.
I squatted, pushed, and let out awful groans.
Years before, I saw Michelangelo's
unfinished statues, those torsos of men
pulling themselves from rough blocks of stone.
Love, in those first few moments that I spent
as your mother, while you flailed and shone,
beautifully formed and finally free,
I tell you, what I felt like was debris.

New Mother Reading

Ona Gritz

Make of Yourself a Light by Hannah Wilson

The poem says the Buddha said
make of yourself a light...
That is all. I am relieved
of the need to be Good,
to be Wise, to be Other.
All I need do is walk ahead
so my children can see
into the dark.

We have been here past an hour,
a book in my hand, the weight
of my son's head warming
the crook of my arm. His mouth,
slack against my breast, breathing
inaudible. On the page,
the poem says the Buddha said
make of yourself a light...

The light has shifted to gray
but I'm anchored, the switch
for the lamps out of reach. Downstairs,
someone is tending a shop. Bagging fruit,
making change. For now, I am absolved
of that kind of work. My job, love.
That is all. I am relieved
of the need to be good.

The need for milk wakens in him.
Eyes closed, he searches
with gums and tongue. Here
is what I want for him. Ease
in his body, buoy for a heart,
splashes of laughter.
To be wise, to be other.
All I need do is walk ahead

the poem says. But I think
next to for a good while,
and later, *behind.* For now,
I feel milk release, hear the wet
sounds of my son's working throat.
He blinks and squints up at my face
as though it shines for him
through the approaching dark.

Far More Hers Than His

Peter Austin

When John and Liz's firstborn died of SIDS
And, five years on, their hopes of more had flopped,
Instead of giving up on having kids
They chose to go to China and adopt.
Another expedition, then a third
And, lo! they were a family of five
Whose mother was routinely overheard
Declaring them the happiest alive.

But John, at forty, fell in love with Kate
(Nineteen of course) and told the shattered Liz
That she could have the car and real estate
And — well, the girls *were* far more hers than his….
He's father, now, to Joey, Jeff and Jim
Who (everybody says it) look like him.

French Braids

Robert W. Crawford

While one hand is content to touch, admire
A balanced, careful weave — preserve for viewing
The beauty and the boundaries of desire —
The other hand is busy at undoing.
The quiet hand counsels restraint; afraid
To wreck the composition of composure,
It's wary of destruction just for fun.
The other wants to slip between each braid,
To tease apart the strands, let run, spill over,
Release, unbind, what was so neatly done.
Your urgent kiss decides which hand is played.
A gentle pull brings argument to closure.
Surprised, my hands attempt to catch your hair:
It falls the way the rain lets go the air.

Previously appeared in *The Cumberland Review*

Summer Island

Michael Cantor

You sit outside, consorting with your wine
as I, inside, consider what to say
or do to try to redefine the line
you sit outside. Consorting with your wine
now seems your choice; and solitude is mine,
and neither works to overcome the way
you sit outside, consorting with your wine
as I, inside, consider what to say.

Sestina for an Ending

Kendall A. Bell

Each slab of paving holds a film of dirt.
A humid sky: the air is not yet cold.
Her boots press footprints into the grass cover;
she pauses, wipes her brow, and drinks some water,
glances up — thick clouds, one break of light —
and sighs an accusation with no answer.

Inside, a phone is ringing without answer;
outside, she rakes the earth to break the dirt.
This soil is nutrient poor, its color, light;
this fruitless ritual hers. To keep out cold
she tends her plants. They have long needed water,
and as it comes, she darts to the garage for cover.

After the rain, she gets a light coat to cover
her tired body. She mutters with no answer,
retreats indoors eventually for more water.
She sees her footprints, written on the floor in dirt,
thinks of her husband: how their union went cold.
She drops to the sofa, turns out the only light.

Miles away, he drives in brighter light.
He took the day off; a friend agreed to cover.
He does not like to be controlled, a cold
fury builds; he says, "She was never the answer.
She wants me six feet under covered in dirt."
He drives until he can see the ocean's water.

He walks over sand forever, reaches the water,
pale skin already burning in strong light.
This is the last time she'll treat him like dirt,
he thinks. He'll vanish: no trace to recover.
If his phone rings, he'll ignore its shriek, not answer.
He enters greenish water, getting cold.

He cannot bear her silence and the cold.
After a brief swim he stumbles out of the water.
But is the search for another really the answer?
He swaps his towel for a cigarette, looks for a light.
Maybe she has mountains more to discover,
more depths to mine. He speeds off in a cloud of dirt.

He calls and calls: no answer. She's quit him cold.
Soon after, another tracks in dirt, rainwater
and lets in light, his arms, the sweetest cover.

Your Missing Piece

Bruce W. Niedt

Like a puzzle, you now feel incomplete,
afraid to let me see the angry scar
where it was sliced away like so much meat.
You wonder what is left, and what you are—
asymmetry that makes a restless night.
You worry I'll no longer hold you close,
but you're my source, my beacon of delight.
You're, in my eyes, a pruned but perfect rose.

Reminding us of our mortality,
events like this can forge a stronger bond,
a love unfazed by stark reality,
that rides the rapids for a quiet pond.

The bottom line is, it was just a breast;
the best news is, we get to keep the rest.

Youth Politic

High Heel

Erica Dawson

I was born, Mom says, bull's eye
Parfait, without a flaw — reflex
And one repro of fine she-sex —
All lash and rock-a-bye —

Full lids looking to close.
Slim collarbone, and rosebud pout,
I'm Queen without a Doubt
Of all hatched embryos.

Long may I reign with a spine
Perfected in its curvature's
Half curlicue and constant manicures
On two flat feet. I line

My ankles up and, see,
They propinquate. They roll until
They collapse. The missing insteps spill
From the slingbacks' nudity

And barest ties. So call
Me Mary Jane with a turf toe fetish.
I'm stacked. With three-inch-high coquettish
Stilettos, I'm Belle o' the Ball

And socket joint. There goes
High Heel. I've heard my ankles crack
And traced the point where I go black
To white on all ten toes

(Top brown to bottom peach)
As if my foot's biracial. In
The lady's pump, I'm genuine
Sunday Best (Praise Jesus! Preach!).

I'm the club's platforms. And though
I'll never arabesque en pointe,
I stand, bipodal, to disappoint
With all this bod, dance the foe

's faux pas de deux with the full-
Length mirror. I'm patent, polished, buffed,
Strap-bound, and muled. I'm powderpuffed.
I'm pinched. With a push and pull,

I make my blisters pop
In a serous ooze. If I could name
The foot's small bones, I'd play a game
And count the talus, cop

The dice and cuneiform,
The mid-foot characters (the wedges
Somewhere beneath the thong's thin edges),
The cuboid, and linguiform

Long toes in dual tones.
My skeleton is narratory,
Completely born and half a story
Writ large in genes and bones.

Joy Ride

Catherine Chandler

I cheated death — oh, what a thrill! —
that summer afternoon I sped
my brand-new Schwinn down Beaumont hill
right through the stop sign, and instead

of braking, met a fateless day.
Why did I do it? I was one
who brushed her teeth, put toys away,
but thought some freedom might be fun.

And so it was, till guilt set in:
grim thoughts — a crowd, a mangled waif,
my disobedience, a sin
I never did confess.
                           It's safe

to be an easy rider; blah
to take the road most traveled by.
For years now I've obeyed the law.
But once I was a butterfly.

Miss Ross

Chris Bullard

Miss Ross had gotten all of us confused
when she suggested Housman meant to play
upon our sense of words. "See how he used
the phrase, "Smart lad to slip betimes away."
Is "Die young," what he meant, or does he say
the opposite of that?" The classroom sighed.
To us it didn't matter either way.
Was there a runner? Had he really died?
For all we knew about it, Housman might have lied.

Miss Carmen Ross was tall, red-haired and not
the sort of teacher found at our high school.
No one else would startle us with crackpot
suggestions, nor ask questions that might fool
you into answers. And her ridicule,
however gentle, made her students fear
to give a dull response. Surely, some rule
said teachers shouldn't ask, " Would you hear
me better, if I were to bite you on your ear?"

We stared off through the safety tinted glass
to what the future parked for us outside.
"Does Frost want us to invest in bonds? Class?
What was he saying in Provide, Provide?"
Was it our silence that dissatisfied
Miss Ross, or the senior in the first row
who, lounging back, Beatle-coiffed and tie-dyed,
asked how it was that anyone would know?
If that was what he thought, why couldn't he just say so?

"Didn't Frost do just that? Don't his words connote
much more than what they say literally.
If everything that Frost or Housman wrote
was so simply taken that it could be
summed in a phrase, we'd watch it on TV;
no need to read when poets could just knit
up samplers of sentiment. Irony
is light upon those sins our words commit—
those sins we pass along when teaching English Lit."

Miss Ross dismissed us. We went out to lie
in unambiguous sunlight. A few
good boys, for country, would enlist to die
in Asia. Some would fumble out, "I do,"
and yet, would not. Others would be true
to household gods and goods. O Fairy Queen
of my dumb youth, I would now invoke you
against this literal world, by imagining
a language meaning more than words might mean to mean.

Paintball Loser

Michael Battram

Whatever age he was, he looked too small
for it, but I figured age of ten.
A paintball gun swung limply from his hand
as he walked down the street. His hair and face
were soaked with lurid colors—I thought, man,
They must have ganged up big-time on this kid,

his so-called "friends," no doubt. Were they just kidding
around at first, they told themselves, these smaller
versions of the shits they'll be as men
someday? And I wondered, has this happened often?
How many times has he had to face
some double-cross, then watched those boys' glad-handing

and high-fives? Does he rise from sleep with hands
balled up in fists and swinging at those kids,
bloodying their stupid laughing faces
in his dreams, for making him feel small
and weak? It's tough—a boy by the age of ten
is too old to cry, too young for any woman

but his mother. Does he know that women
hold our entire world within their hands,
they carry the sky upon their backs, too often
feeling burdened as any bullied kid?
I hoped his mom could comfort him, in small,
sweet ways, at least: fix lunch or wash his face,

anything to give him courage facing
one more day. So many boys, and men,
without this courage, someday become just small
and petty tyrants, who never raise their hands
except at home, against their wives, or kids—
my God, you'd have to have a heart of tin

to feel no pity. I think of that boy often,
hoping he will see some lovely face
each day he lives, someone who'll say, "Don't kid
yourself, it isn't easy, being a man,
and in this world, life will never hand
you much," who'll make him more than just some small

and picked-on, defeated kid with a paint-smeared face,
who'll give his hands and heart the strength of ten,
this small boy, waiting to become a man.

Summer Ice

Penny Harter

The ice-man entered through the kitchen door,
his sharp tongs biting hard into a chunk
of blue-green ice, then dropped it in the sink
as sawdust spilled onto the dripping floor.
He hoisted in another piece or two,
then carried them across the room to stack
them in the icebox where a dwindling block
had melted down into a milky stew.
We felt the heat buzz hard against the house
like angry insects beating to get in,
and all the fan blades whirred against the sun
while Nana wiped her forehead on her blouse.
And sometimes I would reach inside to touch
those frozen slabs of lake that came to us.

Jimmy Carter, King of America

Quincy R. Lehr

I must have been—what?—four when Jimmy Carter
stepped out of Air Force One on the TV set,
smiling and shaking hands despite the polls
and all the shit that must've been going down.
There were exorcisms in Tehran,
with "Death to the Great Satan!" on the lips
of mullahs, while the Soviet helicopters
swarmed Afghanistan. But I was four
and didn't know quite who the hell it was
waving at us, so I asked my Mom.

"That's Jimmy Carter, Quincy." But who's he?
"The leader of our country." Oh, our *king*.
I'd heard the fairy tales and thought I knew
the ins and outs of war and politics.
But he didn't look that regal in a suit
like something that my Dad would wear to church.
No crown or scepter—and what was with the surname?
Kings had numbers, or really awesome titles
like "Lionheart," "the Mad," "the Third," "the Bold,"
"the Great"—or even "the Magnificent."

I went outside and played catch with my Dad,
who laughed when I explained what I had learned
about our king. But grown-ups always laughed
(or so it seemed) at my discoveries—
that the sky was far too high to reach,
even for them, that toilet water swirled
the same direction every time you flushed,
that snow was frozen rain. I let him laugh,
and then my Dad and I went in to eat
the supper that was always on the table.

King Carter was replaced by Ronald Reagan—
who had a different last name, and was older.
I learned about elections, the tradition
of voting on a Tuesday for our leaders—
all citizens "like us." But soon enough,
I heard of Contras out in jungles, islands
swarming with Marines… and slavery,
homeless people, and laid-off auto workers,
and that our TV came from far away,
a place whose name I couldn't quite pronounce.

You can't go back, of course. The TV set
is in some dump in central Oklahoma.
A different generation's in the yard
of the house my mother sold when she dumped Dad.
I've also learned that you don't need a king
to have an empire, court, and sycophants
while the poor get screwed, and every day, the news
comes like a tedious joke, in sober suits,
straight-faced insanity that we switch off,
then heat a frozen dinner from the fridge.

Collateral Damage

Robert Klein Engler

The state sets up long rows of concrete chairs.
We knew in Vietnam that babies died.
With Zyklon gas, napalm and ash of hairs,
If you are keeping score, I guess we're tied.
The scholars say our Civil War was won,
But who divines the threads of terror's web?
It's June, the baseball season's just begun,
So, please, don't raise the ghost of Johnny Reb.
While polls shift left and right, we wait the bells
That tell again of horror wrecked by one.
Some say we lost our way. Some say death sells.
His stare is steel, then cold. Our job is done.
More blood will never bring an end to blood—
The second end is fire, the first was flood.

Only the Good

Hypochondriacal

Paul Hostovsky

I thought I was dying but it was nothing.
It seems to be happening more and more often.
It's the kind of nothing that's something

the way a coat hanger swinging
in an empty room you keep coming back to
because you think something is in there, is nothing —

the way a current of air,
or a rise in the wind, or an almost imperceptible
drop in the temperature, is something.

Some things are more themselves than others.
Some are lymphomas, and some are lipomas,
and sometimes all the worrying's for nothing —

the fasting, the testing, the blood-work and x-rays,
the invasive, exploratory, tortuous, torturous
procedures turn up nothing. Something

poetic about a lifetime of saying
you're dying. Something hyperbolic.
Something metaphoric. Nothing
like a good metaphor for saying what something's like.

Jane

E. Shaun Russell

She wore no wig to cover her bald head
when first we met—she seemed to feel no shame;
"It's fine…my mom had cancer too," I said.
I saw the words sink in and wished instead
I hadn't said a thing, and not laid blame
on some obtrusive illness—should have read
her face and seen that coping with such dread
depends on never calling it by name.

On the Anniversary of a Natural Disaster

Jennifer Reeser

I found an infant alligator floating
in Perkins' Bayou yesterday, between
Louisiana iris and the green
of blighted summer reeds, its stomach bloating
with harsh, bright, glaring sunlight, without fault
or scale, as crocodiles would have; its head
chin up and oblong, grimacing, as dead
as mausoleum marble, white as salt.

Delight in a discovery so exotic
could not be lost on me, however grim.
Mosquito larvae harbored in a scrim
of water on the western bank, hypnotic
and circling with the rise-and-falling rasp
of locusts at the cypress. In my grasp
a camera – in the case some killer storm
destroys this haunt tomorrow, everything
familiar, safe, replaced by suffering –
chaos projecting fatally through form.

Originally appeared in *Chronides: A Magazine of American Culture*

Pleistocene Relic

Tiel Aisha Ansari

The color of my mind is silence. Wind
through hollow trees and over river beds
of sand and gravel. Seedless thistle heads
adorn the broken teeth that lately grinned
from bleaching skulls on tundra prairies. Dusk
turns air to lavender and earth to grey.
A gap in western clouds; a single ray,
a glimpse of red that glitters on my tusk.

The thunder of my hooves is silent. Sky
fills every crevice in my cranium.
I wait, immobile, for the rain to come
and pool like blueness in my empty eye,
my staring socket, hollow ivory bone
a frame for wooden shaft and fluted stone.

In Dreams

Julie R. Enszer

For Lara

Dear Lara, Do you know Greta still dreams
about you? I don't, which is fine. Your life,
your death reminded me of what is divine:

daily life. Like the pictures that litter my shelves.
Hundreds. All framed. Yet only two of you,
dear Lara. Do you know: Greta still dreams

about you. It worries me. You, dead eight years.
I listen to her dreams, but want to scream, "Move on from
her death! Remind me, what is divine?

The living are divine!" If I did say that and
you, alive, heard it, you would laugh,
Lara. You know Greta. She dreams

big dreams and tries to love them into truth,
which is why, I think, she holds so tightly to
you as if rewinding death, setting back time.

Yet, we know, time only marches forward;
there will be no more pictures snapped of you.
Dear Lara, do you know Greta still dreams
your death. Remind me, again, what is divine?

No

A.M. Juster

No, not this time. I cannot celebrate
a man's discarded life, and will not try;
these knee-jerk elegies perpetuate
the nightshade lies of Plath. Why glorify
descent into a solipsistic hell?
Stop. Softly curse the waste. Don't elevate
his suffering to genius. Never tell
me he will live on. Never call it fate.

Attend the service. Mourn. Pray. Comfort those
he lacerated. Keep him in your heart,
but use that grief to teach. When you compose
a line, it is a message, not just art.
Be furious with me, but I refuse
to praise him. No, we have too much to lose.

Selected by Frederick Turner as winner of the 2006 Howard Nemerov Sonnet Award. Published in *Measure*.

Reproof

Frank Osen

I have no other resource than this irony: to speak of the "nothing to say."
ROLAND BARTHES, *Camera Lucida*

Up north today to catch a college game
I'm nodding through the running commentaries
of friends recounting all our halt and lame,
when one says you're still hanging out at Perry's.
So afterwards, I go; it's not that far
and sure enough, beyond a row of beers
and spirits, and across a host of years,
your twenty-something picture tends the bar.

It's held its own, if not intensified —
that shock of blond, blue-eyed, electric poise,
worn since by countless Abercrombie boys
but current now, as on the night you died.
It's kept your image on that wall, iconic,
where memory and snapshot might concur
that at some other point in time, you *were* —
before the blurred one adds its own ironic

And then, you weren't — the accident, that spring
you worked here, fresh from school, was all your fault
and no surprise; we'd seen how you'd assault
the hills in your MG — a driven thing.
At least you never dreamed you'd maim
somebody, let alone the crash would claim
in slower motion, but every bit as wild,
your parents, who'd lost their only child.

Now, gray as they were, past the young bud's day-

long grief, the silliness of a bouquet,
silly all by myself, I stand composed
as an absurdly late eyewitness, posed
with, if not yours, still no one else's face.
Here in this fine and private public place
and feel the impact like a passerby —
to know you're dead, but see you yet to die.

Sonnenizio Sessantina

Maryann Corbett

That time of year thou may'st in me behold
when bits quit holding up; things fall apart.
"The center will not hold!" the doctors scold.
The surface, either. Holdouts ply their art—
cosmetics, dye—but those won't hold at bay
brute forces, no holds barred. The tissues fold up
like blown umbrellas. Mind-hold steals away:
It's less a gentle cheat than a gunpoint holdup.
You're pigeonholed now. *Matron.* Even *hag.*
You're jaded reader, holed up with Qoheleth.
You've held so long—the line, the key, the bag—
that all you're holding, finally, is a breath.
Held over, pending, idled, space unsold.
And still the phone recordings sigh: *Please hold.*

Whiskey Tango Foxtrot

Jehanne Dubrow

— what the fuck?

Foxtrot the Navy, I yell into the phone,
the first time that my husband groans *deployed*,
a word we've waited for since war began
four years ago.
                    Let *whiskey* slide as slow
as bullets down my throat. Let *foxtrot* be
both verb and noun.
                    Foxtrot the Navy,
I say again but softer than before,
as if the whisper of a dance could keep
him here.
                    I need a shot of *whiskey* just
to take the news, a song in 2/4 time
and rhinestone shoes.
                    Foxtrot, I sigh —
third time's the charm in everything but war,
oh ugly, big sublime. I'm buzzing with
white noise.
                    Call in the dancing girls,
the boys who swallow slugs from Jerry cans,
moonshine sloshed to the brim of each canteen.
Let *whiskey* taste toxic as benzene.

from *Stateside* (Northwestern UP, 2010)

Church Going

Chips & Queso

Mike Alexander

Your table's set with chips & *queso*,
& guacamole's on the way.
The best in town; the guidebooks say so.
Your table's set with chips & *queso*;
as long as the dollar outpaces the peso,
you can relax. Enjoy your stay.
Your table's set with chips & *queso*,
& guacamole's on the way.

The waiter with the smiling eye
knows you & all your kind are rich,
for he has seen what you can buy.
The waiter with the smiling eye
believes that God will rectify
all debts when meek & mighty switch.
The waiter with the smiling eye
knows you & all your kind are rich.

He doesn't know about the pills
you take to regulate your heart
or keep in check your nightly chills.
He doesn't know about the pills,
the credit margin, the unpaid bills,
why your marriage fell apart.
He doesn't know about the pills
you take to regulate your heart.

The so-called harmony of the spheres
rings equally for everyone,
but since nobody really hears
the so-called harmony of the spheres,

the fault must lie with human ears.
Tone-deaf, we howl beneath the sun.
The so-called harmony of the spheres
rings equally for everyone.

Peals of prayer roll hot & wet
from bells in the cathedral tower,
whose belfries open wide, to let
peals of prayer roll hot & wet
across your face, till you forget
how strange it is, at twilight hour:
Peals of prayer roll hot & wet
from bells in the cathedral tower.

On the far side of the street,
a dusty taxi's polychrome
chimes back. Say grace, & start to eat.
On the far side of the street,
the colors of the day compete.
El Sol invites you to his home
on the far side of the street:
a dusty taxi, polychrome.

A mariachi's big sombrero
shines down its blessing, a man
wearing the mask of a lone *vaquero*,
a mariachi's big sombrero,
singing, *Yo no soy marinero,*
soy Capitan, soy Capitan…
A mariachi's big sombrero
shines down its blessing. Amen.

A Second Eden?

T.S. Kerrigan

I pause along these coastal cliffs,
When Garryowen stops to sniff
A heap of Eucalyptus leaves,
And think of bronzed seafaring men
From islands lying south of here,

Those Polynesians, ages past,
Who navigated miles of sea
In fleets of flimsy hand-hewn craft,
Without a compass, gyroscope,
By rhythms of the earth and sky.

Invested with that knowledge once,
What made us yield the pagan link
With earth, make blind the hidden eye?
Was erring mankind dispossessed?
Were we cast from the garden twice?

Empty Confessional

Kate Bernadette Benedict

Cellar, attic, I've searched everywhere.
Where is the child I conceived in Nonce Garden?
Eras ago, it was; memories harden.
Cellar, attic, I've searched everywhere,
the abandoned tavern, the deserted square,
this sterile church where I've come for pardon.
Cellar, attic, I've searched everywhere.
Where is the child I conceived in Nonce Garden?

Up

Tiel Aisha Ansari

Where were you when the fires rose up?
Where is the image before it shows up?

Seeds are deep-buried, far from the light,
somehow the shoot germinates and knows up.

Where did the sundial's shadow disappear to?
Clocks wind down and a child grows up.

Tell me if you know the final answers
why stones fall and water never flows up.

Where has yesterday's caravan gone,
footprints hidden by the dust that blows up?

Shopkeepers shut their doors and windows
sun's going down and it's time to close up.

I am dust and a shadow walking.
Call me, Lord, as my spirit goes up.

In His Beak an Olive Branch

Aaron Poochigian

Come, chosen ones, admire the pigeon:
urban and secular, he perches
   on houses of religion,
mosques and synagogues and churches.

When mounted upon Mark the Lion
he coos no Latin to the lambs
   and thinks nothing of Zion
when settling its hexagrams.

Pillared in aniconic space
he rules his roost and cannot care
   which way the faithful face
or what name hastens them to prayer.

Mecca, Jerusalem and Rome —
so much gibberish to a brain
   deprived of words for "home,"
"hereafter," "sacred" and "profane."

Whichever God we wield as judge,
the pigeon never takes offense
   and so can't bear a grudge.
Come, friends, envy his innocence.

The Smokers

Ray Pospisil

The smokers gaze beyond our world and dream
of somewhere distant from the marble stairs
in winter's cold. An exile tribe that shares
the fire in huddled clans, the smokers seem
awaiting some deliverance from the flights
of steps. Inhaling stokes a flame to send
out signals of distress that quickly spend
their heat and dwindle down to votive lights,
while smokers offer scorched and ruined breath
in desperate sacrifice. Their exhales merge
like choir notes. Though packs they carry test
their faith by threatening damaged heirs or death,
the many scattered acolytes converge
in some communion which the ash has blessed.

The Watching

Paul Christian Stevens

*They are most commonly insensible, and feele neither pin, needle, aule, &c. pryked
or thrust through them ... They were watched, only to keepe them waking: for
indeed when they be suffered so to couch, immediately comes their Familiars into
the room and scareth the watchers, and heartneth on the Witch ...*
– Matthew Hopkins, Witch-Finder General, *The Discovery of Witches*

A flicker of quick shadow in the eye's
Corner speaks more proof to me than volumes
Bound in red leather, set in neat array;
One imp of connotation infallibly
Points where no goodwife, under her husband's hand,
Should be revealed complaisant to the letch:
Points out the third teat luring Vinegar Tom,
Hop and Pyewacket to her secret parts.

Naked, awake, watch through our nights and days
To learn that one, true syllable you know
You long to say. My prick about your body
Scribes thick insensible from bright agony,
Thrills out the sweetest spot, that compact zone
You struck with him you never could deny.

Hair of the Dog

David J. Rothman

"News got you down again?" my old friend said,
As he slid into the booth across from me.
The local café. Breakfast. Fresh-baked bread,
Bacon and eggs, good coffee, refills free.
And spilling like cold blood out of the *Times*,
Today's glut of articulate ugliness —
The clichéd round of triggers, sighs and dimes —
A planet's accusations and distress.
He shrugs, reaches and plucks a sorry grape.
"You know…" he says, pausing to chew and swallow,
"…It's just a matter of time. There's no escape."
He smiles. A dog-eared deck fills his hand's hollow.
He says, "The cold, dark house will always win.
Surely…" "Shut up," I say, "just deal me in."

For Art's Sake

Self-Portrait, Age Ten

Susan McLean

After our fifth-grade teacher had us draw
pictures of ourselves, which she displayed
on the wall, I glowed with pleasure when I saw
that mine was nearest the truth. I had conveyed
my sleeveless shirt and pleated skirt, brown eyes
and yellow hair, of course, but best of all,
the parts were roughly of the proper size,
the head and limbs not overlarge nor small.
But when I saw Elizabeth's sketch, I froze,
dismayed. Her head was larger than her body,
with huge blue eyes, a rosebud mouth, no nose,
small feet, and a wasp waist. She looked a beauty
and I looked like a chunky child. I burned,
stung by this vision out of all proportion,
half baby and half Barbie. How had she learned
to draw like that? Could beauty be distortion?
Was it her mom, the hairdresser, who'd taught her?
Mine was a chemist. Fighting off the blues,
I studied the techniques I'd never use—
not lovely but precise, my mother's daughter.

Guns 'N Roses

Austin MacRae

Axl was my god in seventh grade,
a bullied small kid's king of balls-out rock.
I screamed "I wanna watch you bleed!" and prayed
that Slash would murder every asshole jock.
I inked my wimpy bicep with a bic,
armed myself with blooms and barbed-wire vine.
I dreamed my razor coils would snag a chick,
her throbbing heart ensnared by my design.
Listening to "Sweet Child O' Mine" tonight,
I feel a blossom desperate to break free
below that old destructive appetite
to fuck the system manually, to be
blunt and beautiful, to get real pissed
and leave a rose each place I plant my fist.

Sleeping Hermaphrodite

James S. Wilk

Roman copy after work attributed to Polykles of Attica - ca. 160 B.C.,
Paris, Musee du Louvre

How peacefully you sleep! Your sinuous form
has cast aside the bed sheets to reveal
smooth marble skin, as sultry as a warm
Aegean night. Midnight voyeurs, we steal
a glimpse of rounded breast as you embrace
the pillow where you rest your youthful head
and slender neck. Aroused, our gazes trace
your torso, spine and rounded hips, your bed
yielding, like us, to each delicious curve.
Not sated by the sinews of your thighs,
your calves and feet, but starving to observe
what men desire, we shift to glimpse what lies
between your nubile loins and gasp in shock
when we behold your stiff, tumescent cock.

Ballerina

Frank De Canio

Although I make believe I'm nonchalant
while watching arabesques at the ballet,
my pulse so quickens when a girl's en pointe,

I feel just like a giggling debutante
who's carried (metaphorically) away.
Although I act as if I'm nonchalant,

I'm titillated if the girl should flaunt
her pirouettes and sassy relevés.
As my pulse quickens when the girl's en pointe,

her attitude, with foot croisée devant,
unfolds the leg to suave développé.
And though I make believe I'm nonchalant,

my lungs expand with her grand battement
and blissfully expel with the plié.
Oh God! My heart's set on pied a pointe

to distraction. What matter that I can't
do more than just adore the fleet bourées
of dancing feet while I seem nonchalant?
My pulse still quickens when a girl's en pointe.

Mardi Gras Mannequin

Jennifer Reeser

Sequined braiding, gold lamé, split-tunic dress,
kohl-brimming lids and brows, a pythoness
of claret paint down one cheek—who would guess

she'd see such losses in one life, her tulle
a multi-glittered crown of thorns, the jewel
of mysticism round her neck: a fool.

No caricature, though, each feature fine
and delicately handled, she is wine
not punch; not Judy—Judith in design,

expensive and articulate. Trace hands
bend cryptically from crystal-tinseled bands
of cape, expression no one understands.

This is how society begins:
benign impulses, masquerade, mock sins;
loose, thick-skinned drums, horn-blowing chamberlains,

though she might rather credit the ascetic,
the purple of her headdress net pathetic
and purged in its restraint, at the cosmetic

creases of her temples. This is how
society must end, as well—low-brow
or high, with jest and joker, cat's meow

and costumed dog, clown's bow and crowd appeal.
Who could have known the mirth she could make real?
Who the swaths of sorrow she'd conceal,
swan-drawn, eyes streaming burgundy and teal?

Originally appeared in *The Raintown Review*

Casablanca

Clay Stockton

25 May 2006

Originally, in the Epsteins' script,
the last scene showed how Rick and Ilsa fled,
leaving Laszlo behind, as good as dead,
and leaving us to witness how corrupt
true love could be—how acting on the good
(the role love plays in any other film)
was tantamount, in this one, to a crime.

But the dictates of *want* gave ground to *should*
as Victor Laszlo and his wife took flight
to Portugal, from there to greater danger,
while Major Strasser lay inside the hangar,
shot in cold blood and glorious black and white.
How simple it was, knowing what to do,
in the good old days of 1942.

Dolphin Weather

Rick Mullin

A kelp of stones, the crack of ocean's kill
In sun and severed oxygen install
A quorum in the splinter of a gill.

The labor of a morning torn and shrill
By crab and crab gull at the water's wall —
The kelp of stones, the crack of ocean's kill

Along the rolling pile of salted krill —
Describe a howling tear, a wind to call
A quorum in the splinter of a gill.

At crest, the monarch lifts its sail to till
The shadows in its leaden rays, to trawl
The kelp and stone. The crack of ocean's kill

Redounds to dolphin weather in the thrill
Offshore, the bounding in the tidal haul,
A quorum in the splinter of a gill.

A crystalline assemblage, codicil
To codes unfolding, hollowed in the maul
Of kelp and stone, where cracking oceans kill
A quorum in the splinter of a gill.

Peter Austin

All Clear

Grey sea, grey sky,
Rain, in sudden volleys,
Poster, moulting from a wall,
The last of *Lulu's Follies*.

Gulls' mew, surf's boom,
Sigh, and suck, and rattle;
Driftwood, littering the sand
Like bones of vagrant cattle....

Gone the rock, the candy floss
The salty picture postcards,
Sea cadets with jangled tins:
"Support your local coastguard!"
Lusty cheering on the beach
At Punch contusing Judy,
Jetty crammed with crabbers and
Their cacogenic booty;
Gone Miss Lulu's gartered girls,
The stunt men and the comics,
Making fun of wives and sex
And hair-restoring tonics;
Gone the *trommelfeuer* of pop,
The funfair's brazen dazzle,
Clangor of calliope
And rollercoaster's brattle....

Full moon, rising,
Veiled, remote, patrician,
In the west a thread of light,
Magenta, yellow, titian.

All - clear - all - clear,
Winks a beacon, drolly;
Summer's pandemonium
Is changed to something holy.

[*Trommelfeuer* is German for barrage.]

Literally Speaking

A Meditation on Dactylic Hexameter

Maryann Corbett

....forsan et haec olim meminisse juvabit....

This is dactylic hexameter. This is the meter I learned about
back when I first studied Vergil, much longer ago than I'll tell you.
I tell of a lesson that failed; I sing of a student who stumbled.
"This, even this, one day, will be helpful for us to remember...."
That's what the poet said, anyway.

Think of a scratchy recording, a thirty-three rpm relic,
and under the scratches and crackles, a basso declaiming *Evangeline:*
"This is the forest primeval, the murmuring pines and the hemlocks" —
that was to show us the meter of *Arma virumque cano* –
and beating it out on the table,

the hand of an elderly teacher, her finger-joints lumped and arthritic.
Think of old Longfellow's poem, unread now for so many decades.
Think of old classrooms, old desks, old textbooks with fray-cornered covers.
Feel the great age of the Latin, and all this antiquity pressing
on us who were girls of sixteen.

Soothing old rhythms and sounds, but the road where they led me dead-
                                                                    ended.
English is different from Latin, and stresses are different from long-marks.
Scattered and careless, I fumbled the Latin idea of duration.
(Lord, how I cringe when I think of the ways I misscanned the *Aeneid,*
misunderstanding the sound of it.)

A wonder it happens at all, that young people learn from old epics.
So many ways of mishearing the rustle of papery voices.
Still, there are fragments that stick; we look for them later and find them.
"Tears of things": now that I've shed them, the line that most comes to me
                                                                    lately —

memory speaking in dactyls.

Letter for Emily Dickinson

Annie Finch

When I cut words you never may have said
into fresh patterns, pierced in place with pins,
ready to hold them down with my own thread,
they change and twist sometimes, their color spins
loose, and your spider generosity
lends them from language that will never be
free of you after all. My sampler reads,
"called back." It says, "she scribbled out these screeds."
It calls, "she left this trace, and now we start" —
in stitched directions that follow the leads
I take from you, as you take me apart.

You wrote some of your lines while baking bread,
propping a sheet of paper by the bins
of salt and flour, so if your kneading led
to words, you'd tether them as if in thin
black loops on paper. When they sang to be free,
you captured those quick birds relentlessly,
yet kept a slow, sure mercy in your deeds,
leaving them room to peck and hunt their seeds
in the white cages your vast iron art
had made by moving books, and lives, and creeds.
I take from you, as you take me apart.

"A Letter for Emily Dickinson" is reprinted from CALENDARS (Tupelo Press, 2003).

Das Mädchen ohne Hände

Mike Alexander

The angels interfere too much.
They think to meddle is divine;
they tinker with my grand design,
whittling at it notch by notch.

They see a pretty young *fraulein*
who's lost her arms to some debauch.
Without her arms she cannot clutch
the fruit that dangles off the vine.

Without her arms she cannot touch
the part that makes of man a swine.
But O these angels of the Rhine,
they do not offer her a crutch.

They do not care they cross the line,
or whose fine narrative they botch:
new silver hands, explicit crotch,
a marriage bed, a noble wine.

This story's ending turned benign.
God damn the angels that kept watch.
That changeling child, that bridal catch,
the girl was promised me. She's mine.

Houseguests

A.M. Juster

There's shouting by the stove (it's Plath & Hughes)
as Wystan wanders off without his shoes
and Whitman picks the Cheetos off his beard.
The Larkin-Ginsberg chat is getting weird,
for after countless hours they have found
bizarre pornography is common ground.
Old Emily is not
As prim as billed —
When Dylan finds her bra-hooks —
She is thrilled.
Poe strokes his bird; Pound yawps that it's a pity
Eliot can't sleep without his kitty.
Rimbaud's on eBay searching for a zebra
while sneering, "*Oui,* a *cheemp* can write *vers libre!*"
The Doctor's soggy chickens start to smell
and Stevens has insurance he must sell.
The readings are spectacular, I know,
but is there any way to make them go?

Expansion on Voltaire's Grammar

J. Patrick Lewis

The Adjective is enemy of the Noun,
Which manages precision on its own.
The English language wears a royal crown
Only when Captain Verb ascends the throne.
To be or not *To be?* The answer's clear.
Is/are/was/were and would have been are very
Inimical to melody. The ear
That craves Mozart gets too much Salieri.
A French provincial woman made Flaubert
Distraught for weeks: He searched for that bon mot
A Verb! personifying her affair.
So if you contemplate striking a blow
For elegance in style, do not disturb
The Adjective. It's dead. Long live the Verb.

Wands & Cauldrons

Chris O'Carroll

Hogwarts Academy
Headmaster Dumbledore,
Mentoring teens in four
Wizard school dorms,

Keeps a keen eye on their
Abracadabratude
As they brave occult and
Hormonal storms.

Ballade of Madame Bovary

Gail White

Was it for this I learned to read
And write and bake a cherry pie?
I was romantic—"All I need
Is love!" was my incessant cry.
But girls, however hard you try,
How long you work, how much you fret,
You'll meet the same reward as I—
A country doctor's all you get.

A wife is only fit to breed
Her brats and sing their lullaby.
Oh, had I only given heed
To those sweet nuns who glorify
The Lord in prayer, and daily die,
I might have been a virgin yet.
But marriage makes the world a sty—
A country doctor's all you get.

I learned to do adultery's deed:
I took two lovers—one a sly
And skillful horseman (I the steed
He rode with such an expert thigh).
My second love was sweetly shy,
An easy fish in rapture's net.
But when I needed cash—good-bye!
A country doctor's all you get.

L'Envoi

Girls, never raise your hopes too high.
Lower your standards, and forget
The dream of catching a rich man's eye —
A country doctor's all you get.

The Grimm Girls at 45

Marybeth Rua-Larsen

A Victimology in Fibs

1. Cinderella
Lip.
Trip.
She scolds
the new drip
for his drop in sales.
Her slippers can't compete—she hails
all employees to the factory to re-gild shoes
while her prince sings the blues with her best friend, and she
        schemes to overthrow those Jimmy Choos.

2. Sleeping Beauty
Dip.
Grip.
She helps
him un-zip
beneath the staircase.
No names, just games, electric space
til the school-bell rings. On her way home she picks up pears—
(she tucks seven in the coat she wears), then bakes a sweet and
        sticky mess while music blares.

3. Snow-white
Tip.
Sip.
Twelve-step
program slip.
She's bleached her black hair,
wears dark shades to the ex's fair
so she can see her kids. The dwarves saved her from remand—
bailed her out again—they sigh as she stumbles from the fortune
       teller's stand, flask in hand.

4. Rapunzel
Hip.
Flip.
The prince
likes her whip.
Her hair hits her ass,
shows off her work in the glutes class.
She had her tubes tied and a boob job after the twins
to tempt the pool boy (but she sees him cringe). Then she
       recalls his car payment's due... and grins.

Hamlet in a Hurry

Edmund Conti

To be or not to be
Hamlet of Elsinore
Father dead, uncle king
He felt bereft.

Crazily did in the
Dramatis personae
Characteristic'ly
No one was left.

Forty-Two

What to Do with Your Limbs

Amber Norwood

Hit and run and only Barbie's
legs remain here. Pointed toe made

right for special shoes now flattened,
disregarded in the midday

intersection. Was it anger,
chance disinterest, this perversion?

Boredom, then, or subtle vengeance,
launching plastic bones from open

windows? Bank on mercy. Listen:
all this time spent racing, left leg

leading first then followed, do you
really think your troubles ever

worth concern? How blond our hair or
pink our car, our false careers as

teachers, brides, hygienists, or our
dog walks, racing cars, remodels,

riding horses, or the time we
make to spend on Ken, or naked,

tangled, lost neglected under
beds of growing children. Doesn't

matter. Sometimes, plans are working
to defeat. Conspiracies will

toss your pretty legs from windows.
                    That'll slow the girl down.

Hands

Marybeth Rua-Larsen

To smooth the hair, to hush the lips
To squeeze the flesh below the hips

To feed the fire in small degrees
To test the strength of *no* and *please*

To seize the book, to mark the page
To slam it shut and bar the cage

To spring the bird, to melt the snow
To linger on what too few know

To smudge the ink, to white the lines
To blunt the edge and blur the signs

To skip the stone or fling it wide
To catch what falls or tries to hide

To blind the eyes, to free the will
To pull the trigger or keep still

Crooked Streets

Carol Frith

Time's a calendar of tablet sheets
I fill with notes. Today I walked around
a corner and past a rooming house and found
myself completely lost. The crooked streets
divided, forked like Renaissance conceits.
On every street: the rooming house. A sound
like inland gulls or something crying drowned
out the traffic noise, and pale aesthetes,
anemic ghosts or shades, replaced the men
and women on the street. Like a rhyme
I can't forget, it all comes back again:
the jumbled streets, the rooming house, and I'm
a calendar of tablet sheets, and then
a street, a house, a crooked trick of time.

From *Keepsake Houses: Crooked Streets,* released in 2011 by Finishing Line Press.

The Happy Heart

Lois Marie Harrod

Everyone distrusted the Happy Heart. They
said she was faking her constant content. All those
lemons to lemon liqueur, sour grapes to Beaujolais.
Nothing but a tanked-up Pollyanna, mega-dosing

on Prozac. Every egg in her basket sunny-side up,
rose-colored glasses raging ruby-red, blear-
begone. All her ails to the wind. Someone spied her up
in her attic making a silk hearse out of a sow's tear.

Others spotted her in the middle of the square,
spinning flaws into gold. It had to stop. She was
infecting them all. The barber had began weaving

hair into gloves, the cook turning bones into chairs,
and now the teacher had blown a dull spark
into a feverish flame. Time for quarantine.

The Résumé

Laura Maffei

Not a single slot is left unfilled.
Look how I went from Chase to Merrill Lynch
without a week of temping time unbilled,
and taught six adjunct classes in a pinch
the year the man I married lost his mind.
Oops, that's not on there—nor is how I wound
up broke in Eastern Europe, slumped behind
a concrete block of buildings with the sound
of gravel-popping SUVs nearby,
a sobbing heap of failure and regret
considering the fastest way to die,
to cure my wanderlust for good, and yet
returned to make another cubicle mine:
my life on paper one unbroken line.

Bubbles

Eric Norris

For Chris

They are so hard to catch. These things defy
The laws of physics. Rising from champagne
Flutes, from orchestras, they even fly,
Laughing, from small children. They contain

No real meaning. Bubbles are absurd
Symbolic structures anyone can make
Cheaply from diluted soap. A word
Could not possess less value. If you break

A bubble nothing happens. They don't curse
Or go upsetting seismographs. The skin
Detects a little something — mist — at worst —
A highly localized cloud burst. But in

Some atomic way, all these events
Lead back to a Big Bang. If that makes sense.

A Glimpse

Peter Swanson

Along my street she pedals past,
No plastic helmet on her head,
    Long hair untied and red.
Such incandescence travels fast.

Instead of spandex, pair of jeans.
Instead of crouched, upright.
    She's meant for dappled light,
The rutted path, pastoral scenes.

Most bicyclists these days appall;
With neon shirts and padded ass,
    They look both vain and crass.
She didn't. That was all.

Power Failure

Robert W. Crawford

Groggy, at first, you think a bulb's burnt out.
But, the clock is off. The hum is gone.
An unfamiliar silence has returned.
Maybe it's just your room, but there's no water.
Maybe it's just the inn, but out the window,
Against the trees, the only light is the snow.
The valley down to Littleton is dark.
And so you wonder how far the failure goes:
This town; a few towns over; or did it start
Beyond the notch, spread all the way from Boston?
Because the silence seems so large, because
It's late at night, you wonder if there might
Have been a great catastrophe that changed
Everything on the other side of the mountains.
Though that would be an ugly, selfish thought,
Standing there looking out the window, and
Feeling the cold creep through the watery glass,
There is, engaged, a part of you — admit it! —
That wouldn't mind the starting all over again;
The desperate part of you that longs
For winter, and a covering of snow.

Previously appeared in *The Formalist*

Biographies

Mike Alexander's first full-length collection, *The Necessary Slice*, is forthcoming from Seven Towers Ltd. (Dublin). A recent chapbook, *We Internet in Different Voices* (Modern Metrics), is available through EXOT books. His poems have recently appeared in *River Styx, Measure, Raintown Review, Abridged, Southword, The Flea* & other journals.

Tiel Aisha Ansari is a Sufi, martial artist, and data analyst living in the Pacific Northwest. Her work has appeared or is forthcoming in *The Bruised Peach, Islamica Magazine, Windfall, Verseweavers, The Lyric, The Barefoot Muse*, and the *VoiceCatcher* anthology from Portland Women Writers. Her poetry has been featured on KBOO, Prairie Home Companion and MiPoRadio, and has been nominated for a Pushcart Prize. Her collection *Knocking from Inside* is available from Ecstatic Exchange. She is online at knockingfrominside.blogspot.com.

Peter Austin is a Professor of English at Seneca College, in Toronto, where he lives with his wife and three daughters. His poems have appeared in many magazines/anthologies in the USA, Canada, the UK and several other countries. His first collection, *A Many-Splendid Thing*, came out in July 2010. A second collection, *I Am Janus*, will appear early next year. He can be contacted at peteraustin@rogers.com.

Michael Battram is a lifelong resident of Southern Indiana. His poetry has appeared in a wide variety of forms, styles, and publications, from sonnets to prose poems, academic to "ashcan," and he thinks he just might be the only living poet to have been in both *The Lyric* and *Wormwood Review*.

Kendall A. Bell's work has appeared in numerous print and online journals, most recently *Decompression* and *Drown In My Own Fears*. He was nominated for Sundress Publications' Best of the Net collection in 2007, 2009 and 2011. His current chapbook, his eleventh, is called *The Forgotten*. His newest manuscript is *Paper*

Cuts and Iodine, which is looking for a place to land while he continues work on the next one. He is president and a co-founding member of the Quick And Dirty Poets, founder and co-editor of the online journal *Chantarelle's Notebook* and the publisher/editor of Maverick Duck Press. His website is www.kendallabell.com and his chapbooks are available through www.maverickduckpress.com.

Kate Bernadette Benedict is the author of the poetry collections *Here from Away* (2003) and *In Company* (2011). She lives in the Bronx, New York, where she edits the online poetry journals *Umbrella* and *Tilt-a-Whirl*.

Kim Bridgford is the director of the West Chester University Poetry Center and the West Chester University Poetry Conference. As editor of *Mezzo Cammin*, she was the founder of The *Mezzo Cammin* Women Poets Timeline Project, which will eventually be the largest database of women poets in the world. She is the author of five books of poetry: *Undone* (David Robert Books); *Instead of Maps* (David Robert Books); *In the Extreme: Sonnets about World Records* (Story Line Press), winner of the Donald Justice Prize; *Take-Out: Sonnets about Fortune Cookies* (David Robert Books); and *Hitchcock's Coffin: Sonnets about Classic Films* (David Robert Books). Her work has been nominated for the Pulitzer Prize, the Poets' Prize, and four times for a Pushcart Prize.

Chris Bullard is a native of Jacksonville, FL. He lives in Collingswood, NJ, and works for the federal government as an Administrative Law Judge. His work appears in the current issues of *Nimrod* and *Harpur Palate* and will appear later this year in *Pleiades, 32 Poems, New York Quarterly* and *Plainsongs*. Plan B Press published his chapbook, *You Must Not Know Too Much*, in 2009. Big Table Publishing will publish his second chapbook, *O Brilliant Kids*, this fall.

Michael Cantor's work has appeared, in *Measure, The Dark Horse, The Atlanta Review, Raintown Review, Margie, Chimaera, SCR,* and numerous other journals, e-zines and anthologies. His honors include the New England Poetry Club Erika Mumford (2006) and Gretchen Warren (2008) Prizes. His collection, *Life in the Second*

Circle, will be published by Able Muse Press in the Spring of 2012. A chapbook, *The Performer*, was published by Pudding House Press in 2007. A native New Yorker, he has lived and worked in Japan, Europe and Latin America, and now lives on Plum Island, north of Boston on the Massachusetts coast.

Catherine Chandler is an American poet, editor, teacher and translator. She completed graduate studies at McGill University, where she lectured in the Department of Languages and Translation for many years. Her poems, essays and translations from French and Spanish have been published in the US, the UK, Canada and Australia. Recipient of the 2010 Howard Nemerov Sonnet Award, and a four-time Pushcart Prize nominee, she is the author of *Lines of Flight* (Able Muse Press), and two chapbooks, *For No Good Reason* and *All or Nothing*. *This Sweet Order*, a collection of her sonnets, is forthcoming from White Violet Press.

Edmund Conti went through his 500 bio notes and couldn't find anything of interest. He hopes to be more interesting in his remaining years.

Maryann Corbett is the author of *Breath Control*, forthcoming from David Robert Books, and the chapbooks *Dissonance* and *Gardening in a Time of War*. She has been a winner of the Willis Barnstone Translation Prize and a finalist for the Morton Marr prize and the Best of the Net anthology. Her poems, essays, and translations appear in many journals in print and online and in the anthologies *Hot Sonnets*, *The Able Muse Anthology*, and the forthcoming *Imago Dei: Poems from Christianity and Literature*. She lives in St. Paul and works for the Minnesota Legislature.

Robert W. Crawford lives in Chester, NH. His second book of poetry, *The Empty Chair*, won the 2011 Richard Wilbur Award. His poem, "The Empty Chair," won the 2006 Howard Nemerov Sonnet Award and his first book, *Too Much Explanation Can Ruin a Man*, was published in 2005. His poems have appeared in *The Formalist*, *First Things*, *Dark Horse*, *The Raintown Review*, *The Lyric*, *Measure*, *Forbes*, and many other publications. He is a trustee of the Robert

Frost Farm in Derry, NH, a long-time member of the Powow River Poets, and founder of the Hyla Brook Poets.

Erica Dawson's collection, *Big-Eyed Afraid*, won the 2006 Anthony Hecht Poetry Prize. *Contemporary Poetry Review* named it Best Debut of 2007. Erica's poems have appeared in *Barrow Street, Blackbird, VQR, Harvard Review, Literary Imagination*, and other journals. She's also appeared in *Best American Poetry, Swallow Anthony of New American Poets*, and other anthologies. R.S. Gwynn chose her work to end *Poetry: A Pocket Anthology (7th edition)*. She's a professor of English and Writing at the University of Tampa, where she also teaches in their new low-residency MFA program. She lives on the water, with her Shih-Tzu-baby, Stella.

Frank De Canio lives in New Jersey, works and relaxes in Manhattan. He is a psychology major, and has written over 1000 poems, most of them sonnets, liberally conceived. A fan of all sorts of music from Bach to Bob Dylan, from Soca to Shakira, from Amy Beach to Amy Winehouse, opera and world music. As poets he cites Dylan Thomas and Sylvia Plath among others. Shakespeare is his consolation. A fan of the liberal arts, he attends a café philo (a philosophy discussion group) in Manhattan.

Jehanne Dubrow is the author of three poetry collections, including most recently *Stateside*. In 2012, Northwestern University Press will publish her fourth book of poems, *Red Army Red*. Her work has appeared in *Poetry, Southern Review, Prairie Schooner*, and *Crazyhorse*. She is the Interim Director of the Rose O'Neill Literary House and an assistant professor in creative writing at Washington College.

Robert Klein Engler lives in Des Plaines, Illinois and sometimes New Orleans. Many of Robert's poems, stories, paintings and photographs are set in the Crescent City. His long poem, *The Accomplishment of Metaphor and the Necessity of Suffering*, set partially in New Orleans, is published by Headwaters Press, Medusa, New York, 2004. He has received an Illinois Arts Council award for his "Three Poems for Kabbalah." Link with him at Facebook.com to see examples of his recent paintings and photographs. Some of his books are available at Lulu.com. Visit him on the web at RobertKleinEngler.com.

Julie R. Enszer is the author of *Handmade Love* (A Midsummer Night's Press, 2010) and *Sisterhood*, a chapbook (Seven Kitchens Press, 2010), and the editor of *Milk and Honey: A Celebration of Jewish Lesbian Poetry* (A Midsummer Night's Press, 2011). She has her MFA from the University of Maryland and is enrolled currently in the PhD program in Women's Studies at the University of Maryland. She is a regular book reviewer for the *Lambda Book Report* and *Calyx*. You can read more of her work at www.JulieREnszer.com.

Annie Finch is the author of six volumes of poetry including *Eve, Calendars, Among the Goddesses: An Epic Libretto in Seven Dreams*, and *Spells: New and Selected Poems*, forthcoming from Wesleyan University Press. She has published several books of poetics focusing on form, including *The Body of Poetry, The Ghost of Meter*, the textbook *A Poet's Ear*, and the anthologies *A Formal Feeling Comes* and *An Exaltation of Forms*. Her music, art, theater, and opera collaborations have been widely produced, and she co-founded Poets Theater of Maine. She directs the Stonecoast MFA program in creative writing at the University of Southern Maine.

Carol Frith, co-editor of *Ekphrasis,* has chapbooks from Medicinal Purposes, Finishing Line, Palanquin Press, Rattlesnake, and Bacchae Press. Her full-length collection was released by David Robert Books in 2010. Her poems have appeared in *Atlanta Review, Seattle Review, Barefoot Muse, Measure, the Formalist, Rattle, Rhino, POEM, Cutbank, Spillway,* and others. She received a Special Mention listing in the 2003 Pushcart Prize Anthology and has been six times a finalist for the Howard Nemerov Sonnet competition.

Ona Gritz is a poet, columnist, and the author of two children's books. In 2007, she won the Inglis House poetry contest and the Late Blooms Poetry Postcard competition. In 2009, she placed second for Lilith Magazine's Charlotte Newberger Poetry Competition. Her poetry chapbook, *Left Standing*, was published by Finishing Line Press in 2005. Ona's essays have been published in numerous anthologies and journals, most recently *The Utne Reader*,

More magazine and *The Bellingham Review*, where she placed second for the 2008 Annie Dillard Award for Creative Nonfiction. She has received eight Pushcart nominations for her work.

Lois Marie Harrod won the 2010 Hazel Lipa Chapbook (Iowa State University) contest with her manuscript *Cosmogony* and her 11th book *Brief Term*, a collection of poems about teachers and teaching, was published by Black Buzzard in March 2011. She teaches Creative Writing at The College of New Jersey.

Penny Harter is published widely in journals and anthologies, and her literary autobiography appears in *Contemporary Authors*. Her books include *One Bowl* (forthcoming, 2012); *Recycling Starlight*, (2010); *The Night Marsh* (2008); *Along River Road (2005)*; *Buried in the Sky* (2002); *Lizard Light: Poems from the Earth* (1998); and *Turtle Blessing* (1996). With her late husband, William J. Higginson, she co-authored *The Haiku Handbook* (25th Anniversary Edition, 2010), and her illustrated children's alphabestiary, *The Beastie Book*, came out in 2009. A Dodge poet, Harter read at the 2010 Dodge Poetry Festival. She has received three poetry fellowships from the New Jersey State Council on the Arts, the Mary Carolyn Davies Award from the Poetry Society of America, and a January 2011 fellowship from Virginia Center for the Creative Arts.

Paul Hostovsky is the author of three books of poetry, *Bending the Notes* (2008), *Dear Truth* (2009), and *A Little in Love a Lot* (2011). His poems have won a Pushcart Prize and been featured on *Poetry Daily*, *Verse Daily*, *The Writer's Almanac*, and *Best of the Net 2008* and *2009*. He works in Boston as a sign language interpreter. Visit him at www.paulhostovsky.com.

Juleigh Howard-Hobson simultaneously writes literary fiction, formalist poetry and genre work, along with essays and articles, purposely skewing the concept of artistic obligation to any single form or movement. Her poetry has appeared in print and online venues in England, Scotland, USA, Canada, Australia, Germany, Norway and Africa, including journals such as *The Raintown Review*, *Mezzo Cammin*, *Worm*, *New Verse News*, *14 by 14*, *The Lyric*, and the anthologies *Poem, Revised* (Marion Street Press), and *Caduceus: The*

Poets at Art Place (Yale University). She is the Assistant Poetry Editor of *Able Muse*.

A.M. Juster is a three-time winner of the Howard Nemerov Sonnet Award. His books include: *Longing for Laura* (Birch Brook Press 2001), *The Secret Language of Women* (University of Evansville Press 2003), *Horace's Satires* (University of Pennsylvania Press 2008), and *Tibullus' Elegies* (Oxford University Press 2012). His translation of Saint Aldhelm's Riddles will be published by the University of Toronto Press in 2013.

T. S. Kerrigan's poetry has been published on both sides of the Atlantic. In England his work has appeared in *Envoi, Acumen* and *Agenda*, and in the American journals, *The Southern Review, The International Poetry Review* and *First Things*. He has two chapbooks published, *Another Bloomsday at Molly Malone's Pub* (The Inevitable Press, 1999) and *The Shadow Sonnets and Other Poems* (Scienter Press, 2006). His first full collection, *My Dark People* (2008) has been a finalist in three major awards and was nominated for the Pulitzer Prize last year. He has a second full collection, *A Homecoming in the Next Parish Over*, coming out in 2012. His work has also been anthologized in Garrison Keillor's *Good Poems* (Viking/Penguin, 2002) and in *Literature and Its Writers* (Bedford/St. Martins, 2006). He is also the former editor of *The Raintown Review*.

Deborah Kreuze makes a living as an editor and writer in Somerville, Massachusetts. She has served on the editorial staff of two national magazines and edited books for major publishing houses. Her poems have been published in a smattering of online literary magazines and been nominated for Best of the Net and the Pushcart Prize.

David W. Landrum lives and writes in Western Michigan. His poetry has appeared in such journals as *Evansville Review, First Things, Turbulence, Orbis*. His chapbook, *The Impossibility of Epithalamia*, is available from White Violet Press. He edits the poetry journal, Lucid Rhythms, www.lucidrhythms.com.

Quincy R. Lehr's poetry and criticism have appeared in numerous venues in North America, Europe, and Australia. His first book is *Across the Grid of Streets*, and he is the associate editor of *The Raintown Review*. He inevitably lives in Brooklyn, where he teaches history.

J. Patrick Lewis is the author of over seventy-five children's picture and poetry books from Knopf, Atheneum, Dial, Harcourt, Little, Brown, Chronicle, Scholastic and others. His adult poetry has appeared in the *Gettysburg Review, New England Review, Dalhousie Review, New Letters, Southern Humanities Review, new renaissance, Kansas Quarterly, Santa Barbara Review, Fine Madness, Sycamore Review, Light*, and many others. He lives in Westerville, Ohio.

Diane Lockward is the author of three poetry books, most recently, *Temptation by Water* (Wind Publications, 2010). Her poems have been included in such anthologies as *Poetry Daily: 360 Poems from the World's Most Popular Poetry Website* and Garrison Keillor's *Good Poems for Hard Times* and in such journals as *Harvard Review, Spoon River Poetry Review*, and *Prairie Schooner*. Her work has also been featured on *Poetry Daily, Verse Daily*, and *The Writer's Almanac*.

Austin MacRae teaches English at Tompkins Cortland Community College. His poetry has appeared in such journals as *Atlanta Review, 32 Poems, Birmingham Poetry Review, Stone Canoe*, and *The Cortland Review*. He was a finalist for the Morton Marr Poetry Prize and is the author of two chapbook collections, most recently *Graceways* (Exot Book, 2008).

Laura Maffei is the author of *Drops from Her Umbrella* (Inkling Press 2006) and the founding editor of *American Tanka* (est. 1996). Her tanka, free verse, and sonnets have appeared in a variety of anthologies and journals, most recently in *The Naugatuck River Review, Mezzo Cammin*, and *Hot Sonnets* (Entasis Press 2011). She was a Michener fellow at The University of Texas at Austin, and teaches writing and literature at a private prep school.

James Scannell McCormick holds a doctorate in creative writing-poetry from Western Michigan University. He currently lives and teaches in Rochester, Minnesota.

Susan McLean is an English professor at Southwest Minnesota State University in Marshall, MN. Her first poetry collection, *The Best Disguise*, won the 2009 Richard Wilbur Award and was published by the University of Evansville Press. Her poems and translations from Latin and French have appeared in *Subtropics*, *Measure*, *The Raintown Review*, *Able Muse*, *Mezzo Cammin*, and elsewhere.

Rick Mullin's poetry has appeared in various print and online journals, including *American Arts Quarterly, Méasure, The Flea*, and *Ep;phany*. His chapbook, *Aquinas Flinched* was published in 2008 by the Modern Metrics imprint of Exot Books, New York. His book-length poem *Huncke* was published in 2010 by Seven Towers, Dublin, Ireland. His epic, *Soutine*, a five-book poem on the life of the painter Chaim Soutine, is forthcoming from Dos Madres Press, Loveland, Ohio. He is a painter and journalist living in northern New Jersey.

Bruce W. Niedt is a beneficent bureaucrat from southern NJ whose poetry has appeared in many publications, most recently *Writer's Digest, The Lyric, Edison Literary Review, Four and Twenty, Spitball, Shot Glass Journal, The Fib Review, US 1 Worksheets,* and *Tilt-a-Whirl*. His awards include the ByLine Short Fiction and Poetry Prize, first prize for poetry at the Philadelphia Writers Conference, and a Pushcart Prize nomination. His latest chapbook is *Breathing Out* (Finishing Line Press).

Eric Norris is the author of two books available on Lulu.com: *Terence,* a comic translation of A.E. Housman's *A Shropshire Lad,* and *Takaaki,* an epic love poem written in the style of Alexander Pushkin. Along with Gavin Geoffrey Dillard, he is co-author of *Nocturnal Omissions*, an epistolary series of poems exploring love, death, time travel, aging, AIDS, sex, religion and reincarnation, published by Sibling Rivalry Press. He is a co-host of the Carmine

Street Metrics Reading Series at The Bowery Poetry Club. Eric lives in New York City.

Amber Norwood writes and teaches in Los Angeles, where she lives with her husband and son. Her poems have been nominated for the Pushcart Prize.

Chris O'Carroll is a writer and an actor. His poems have appeared in *BigCityLit*, *The Chimaera*, *Folly*, *14 by 14*, *Iambs & Trochees*, *LightenUp Online*, *Light Quarterly*, *Literary Review*, *Measure*, and *The Oldie*, among other print and online journals.

Frank Osen lives in Pasadena, California, and works at the Huntington Library. He was born in Yokosuka, Japan and is married, with three children. He is a graduate of the University of California at Berkeley and Loyola Law School. His work has appeared in the inaugural print edition of *The Able Muse* and in *The Dark Horse*, *Unsplendid*, *The Spectator (UK)*, *The Raintown Review*, *Measure*, and the *Evansville Review*. He has won the Best American Poetry series poem award, placed in the *Writers Digest* poetry competition, has been first runner-up for the Morton Marr award, a semi-finalist for the Able Muse Book award, and a finalist in the Howard Nemerov sonnet competition.

Aaron Poochigian earned his Ph.D in Classics from the University of Minnesota in 2006 and now lives and writes in New York City. His translations of Sappho's poems, *Stung With Love*, are now out through Penguin Classics (with a preface by Carol Anne Duffy), and his translations of the Greek astronomical poem Aratus' *Phaenomena* and Aeschylus' *Persians*, *Seven against Thebes*, and *Suppliants* through Johns Hopkins University Press. He has been award a 2010-2011 NEA Grant in Translation. His work has appeared in such newspapers and journals as the *Financial Times*, *Poems Out Loud* and *Poetry Magazine*.

Ray Pospisil died January 28, 2008. He grew up in Union, New Jersey and spent most of his adult life in New York City. Pospisil worked in energy and environmental journalism from 1981 until his death. He often read his poetry for audiences in the East Village and elsewhere in Manhattan. His work has been published by *Lyric, Iambs & Trochees, The Newport Review, The Raintown Review, Umbrella, The Barefoot Muse, Rogue Scholars,* and others. In 2006, his chapbook of poems, *Some Time Before the Bell,* was published by Modern Metrics Press. A posthumous collection, *The Bell,* appeared in 2009.

Jennifer Reeser studied English in Tulsa, Oklahoma, and at McNeese State University. Her poems, scholarly articles, and translations of French and Russian literature have appeared in numerous anthologies. She is the author of *An Alabaster Flask, Winterproof,* and the Shakespearean series "Sonnets from the Dark Lady." She lives amid the bayous of southern Louisiana.

Marybeth Rua-Larsen lives on the south coast of Massachusetts and teaches basic composition and ESL at Bristol Community College. Her poems, essays, flash fiction and reviews have appeared or are forthcoming in *The Raintown Review, Lilt, The Shit Creek Review, The Flea, Measure, Verse Wisconsin, The Nervous Breakdown* and *Newport Review,* among others. She has been a finalist for the Philbrick Award, nominated several times for both the Pushcart Prize and The Best of the Net, and was recently named winner in the Poetry category for the 2011 Over the Edge New Writer of the Year Competition in Galway, Ireland.

David J. Rothman is the Director of the Poetry Concentration with an Emphasis on Versecraft in the low-residency MFA program at Western State College of Colorado (www.formalversemfa.org), and also teaches at the University of Colorado at Boulder and Lighthouse Writers Workshop in Denver. Rothman's volumes of poetry include *Dominion of Shadow, Beauty at Night* and *The Elephant's Chiropractor,* which was a Finalist for the Colorado Book Award, and he edited *The Geography of Hope: Poets of Colorado's Western Slope.* A new volume of poems, *Go Big,* is forthcoming from Red Hen Press. He lives in Boulder with his wife and two rambunctious boys, and he is the pianist in a jazz trio with the unlikely name of "The Unassessable Outcomes."

Over the past few years, **E. Shaun Russell** has had over sixty poems published in a variety of journals including *Rattle, Writers' Journal, The Asheville Review* and *Ellery Queen's Mystery Magazine*, as well as the first six issues of *Think Journal*, for which he was the Featured Poet for the inaugural issue. Though born and raised in Canada, he immigrated to the United States in early 2010 and now lives with his wife, Anna, in southeast Virginia.

Paul Christian Stevens was born in Yorkshire and resides in New South Wales where he teaches historiography and literature to gifted and talented senior high school students. His prime interests in both subjects lie in Tudor and Jacobean studies. He has published poetry and prose in a wide range of print and online venues.

Clay Stockton lives in Oakland, California. The poem included here, "Casablanca," began as a response to an invitation to "write a poem about the war—unless you support the war, in which case don't write at all."

Peter Swanson lives in Somerville, Massachusetts with his wife and cat. He writes poetry and detective fiction. He has recently appeared in *Asimov's Science Fiction Magazine, The Atlantic, Measure, Slant,* and *Umbrella*.

Gail White is the author of three collections of poetry (the latest being *The Accidental Cynic*) and has also edited or co-edited three anthologies (her favorite being *The Muse Strikes Back*). Her new chapbook, *Sonnets in a Hostile World*, is available from Amazon. Her home is in Breaux Bridge, Louisiana, where she lives on Bayou Teche with her husband and cats.

James S. Wilk is a physician in Denver, Colorado, specializing in medical disorders complicating pregnancy. Dr. Wilk's poems have appeared in a variety of literary journals including *The Raintown Review, The Barefoot Muse, Measure, The Dark Horse, Blue Unicorn, Autumn Sky Poetry* and others. He is the author of two chapbooks: *Shoulders, Fibs, and Lies* (Pudding House, 2008) and *The Seven Year Night: Poems of the Medical Training Experience* (Big Table Publishing, 2010).

About the Editor

Anna M. Evans' poems have appeared or are forthcoming in the *Harvard Review, Atlanta Review, Rattle, American Arts Quarterly*, and *32 Poems*. She gained her MFA from Bennington College, and is the Editor of the *Raintown Review*. Recipient of a 2011 Fellowship from the MacDowell Artists' Colony, she currently teaches poetry at West Windsor Art Center. Her chapbooks *Swimming* and *Selected Sonnets* are available from Maverick Duck Press. Visit her online at www.annamevans.com.

www.ingramcontent.com/pod-product-compliance
Lightning Source LLC
Chambersburg PA
CBHW060313050426

42448CB00009B/1817